The Ascending Path

Reflections of A Flower Girl

A Devotional

Shannon R. Hess

House of Acts
Press

Table of Contents

Forward

One night I woke from a dream. I was 5 years old again. I was wearing a lavender satin dress with lace trim. It was the flower girl dress my grandmother made for me for my aunt's wedding. The Lord let me remember the feeling I had preparing for that beautiful day. It was the first time I felt responsible for something important. My "job" was important. I had to drop the rose petals up the aisle so the bride could find her way to the groom. In my mind, this was huge.

When I woke, I knew the metaphor was huge as well. God was asking me to be a flower girl once again, and for a royal wedding. To help create a fragrant path so His bride would draw closer to Him. Over several weeks He showed me what that meant, and how the path is ascending.

Ascend: (verb) to go up or climb higher

My hope is the words in this book do just that, like petals leading the bride to the groom on her wedding day. I pray you follow each petal and allow it to take you higher and closer to the heart of God. That it helps prepare you to become the part of the bride of Christ you are destined to be.

His heart for His bride has not changed. He has not given up on or abandoned her. Jesus is faithful.

I've long been a lover of flowers and words, and the quote "one of God's words is more powerful than 1000 of mine." Though I'm not sure who said it, I agree with it, nonetheless.

I hope, that as a fellow flower lover, you will also become a fellow lover of the word of God. Because friend, it changes everything.

With Love,

Shannon

If you look the

right way, you can

see that the whole world

is a garden.

Frances Hodgson Burnett,

The Secret Garden

In the beginning

I can't really pinpoint when I fell in love with flowers. I come from a long line of flower lovers. I can't see an iris without thinking of my mother. Imagining her as a little girl, with a (sometimes) hard home life, walking through the iris garden her neighbor grew, finding peace and a love for nature all along the way. Even in the hardest seasons in her life, no matter where she lived, she made time to plant flowers. My grandmother, my dad's mom, has always lived in the same house. She moved right in from her mom's house when she married my grandpa and still lives there as I write this. On the east side of the house grows an over 50-year-old lilac bush. The smell and sight of a lilac takes me back to the comfort of her. Her voice, her hug, her smell, and her stable home where she prayed nightly on her knees for her loved ones. We have clipped lilacs for as long as I can remember. My great grandma Mary had a small, cozy cottagelike home with the best hydrangeas and snow-ball bushes you ever saw in your life. Her yard is where I found my first four leaf clover. My great grandma Goldie, my mom's grandma, has peonies growing so perfectly in her yard that they are etched in my mind. The smell and beauty of the ruffle-like petals. All these women grew other flowers, too, but these are the ones that make me think of them.

It is said the common word 'flower' is mentioned something like 159 times in the Bible. It's in a garden we first really get to know God, our Heavenly Father, as Creator. All through scripture, flowers, herbs, trees, fruit, and gardens paint a scene for some of the most powerful moments and messages. We see 4 major gardens in scripture:

- The Garden of Eden- birth, where it began. It says in Genesis, God Himself would descend to walk in the cool of the day in the garden.
- The Garden of Gethsemane- where Jesus often sought comfort and rest and went to pray. It is also where He ultimately surrenders.
- Golgotha, or Calvary in Latin- the scene for the crucifixion and close to the garden tomb where Jesus was laid, only to rise again in victory like He said He would. Resurrection!
- Lastly, the garden paradise to come- final, complete restoration.

Birth, surrender, resurrection, and restoration.

It is no wonder we feel the pull to the dirt to work with our hands and grow things. We are, after all, created in His image.

I can't remember a time when flowers didn't make me feel joy. I recently made a list of things that made me feel the closest to God, and creation is #1, hands down.

I can pinpoint moments in my life that specific wonders in creation have really drawn me closer to our

Heavenly Father and His voice. From the first red rose that bloomed extremely early after our granddaughter's tragic death, to faithful rainbow reminders throughout my sister's last year on earth, to the ocean waves crashing around me and washing my fears away, to mountains calling my name in my dreams and making me strengthen my hind's feet for high places. He takes me to far off lands I never imagined I would see to meet some of the most beautiful people. The majestic pine tree stays evergreen even while shedding and making room for new growth. The bluebird appears out any window when I sit and wonder about real happiness. And oh goodness, those beautiful, cupped flowers bust open on the tulip tree by our pasture. The beautiful daffodils herald the awakening of spring, poking their little heads out of the frozen winter ground first, telling us, "Wake up, wake up, it is time to shed the winter coat and remember that Jesus makes all things new." Creation is never failing, always leaving awestruck wonder in my heart, and a yearning for heaven one day.

I love all flowers and I'm a firm believer a bouquet of flowers on the kitchen table can change the atmosphere in an instant. I dare you to try it. And if you're one of those rare people who don't care about flowers or nature at all, well you probably aren't reading this. But if by chance you are, then I'm praying you stop and take a second look around you, and that look changes for you forever. That you never look at the yellow daffodil growing in a cluster on the side of a road the same way again. That you learn to lean in today and listen to creation always singing His praises.

This book is made up of 24 devotions, full of scripture, and personal stories. You can do it over 24 days or 24 weeks. However you feel led. It is designed to encourage you to ascend higher and closer to Jesus. To help you recognize any unhealthy places in your heart or life that need to be dealt with as you go. It has prayer prompts and journaling areas and original, beautiful artwork by Carmella Calhoun just for this book.

I believe scripture shows us that keeping a record of what God says and does and even how we feel is crucial. He already knows what is in our heart. Thankfully, He meets us where we are, not where we pretend to be or even wish we were. He reveals things to heal them, not to create shame, or unworthiness, or fear, not to camp there and throw a pity party. Remember the Word says:

"And they have conquered him by the blood of the Lamb and by the word of their testimony, for they loved not their lives even unto death"
Revelation 12:11

Keeping a record of feelings helps you see the ones that are not sanctified, the ones lying to you. Because God did give us feelings for a purpose. He feels deeply and so do we. Learning to align our feelings with His is key and is very possible. Then, when you look back, you can see the places God carried you, corrected you, and always loved you. You will see yourself the way He does...

not once a sinner, always a sinner. Not some wretched creature He had pity on. He sees you through the blood of Jesus. He says you are kings and royal priests. He calls you righteous. We may all have descended from a lineage of man, but our goal should be to ascend in our royal lineage as sons and daughters of God. To walk closer with Him.

"Though He descended to walk among us, through His resurrection He ascended back to the Father to make a way, prepare a house, tore the veil so we can now have access through His Holy Spirit to walk closer with God while we live out our purposes."
-Anonymous

1

Winter always ends

"The season has changed, the bondage of your barren winter has ended, and the season of hiding is over and gone. The rains have soaked the earth and left it bright blossoming flowers. The season for shining and pruning the vines has arrived. I hear the cooing of doves in our land, filling the air with songs to awaken and guide you forth."
Song of Songs 2:11-12 TPT

There is this point in winter, a place you could say where we look at the land and it seems nothing will ever grow again. It looks barren, dead, lifeless, even hopeless. But then the rains start, and warm air joins in. It feels stormy, and hard some days. It even feels destructive, but there is promise of life on the horizon.

Winter ends, it always does.

Then you see flowers spring forth from the ground, like little trumpets heralding the end of one season and the start of another like a gentle, loving reminder. He really does make all things new. The flowers can't be rushed or slowed. No, they keep time with heaven's rhythm and bloom when the time is right.

You can, too.

There may be days it's hard to imagine, or seems hopeless, or like nothing will work out. But it will. Trust the One who planted you. You are here in this time and season for a reason.

Pray with me:

Thank You Lord that seasons change, but Your Word does not. And Your Word says You finish every good work you start. Help me, Lord, to see and embrace the plans You created for me to fulfill. To co- labor with Your Holy Spirit to bring it all to life. In Jesus' name, amen.

Declare this:

I trust You Lord, in every season. I trust you.

Bloom now.
Even in the midst of heartache, and questions that come
with change.
The sun comes up and goes down.
The seasons change.
Time waits for no one.
I hope you take a moment to look around you today,
and forgive if you need to, to love and be loved.
Because this life on earth is a vapor.

*"And we all know that for those who love God all
things work together for good, for those who are
called according to his purpose."*
Romans 8:28
(go ahead and read all of Romans 8… it is so good!)

*"for everything there is a season, and a time for
every matter under the heavens"*
Ecclesiastes 3:1

2

Are you using the tools God gave you?

"The ax is already at the root of the trees, and every tree that does not produce good fruit will be cut down and thrown into the fire"
Matthew 3:10

"Jesus replied, 'every plant that my heavenly father has not planted will be pulled up by the roots.'"
Matthew 15:13

One of my favorite ways to hear God speak is working in the garden. As soon as my hands dig in the dirt, or plant a seed, smell the lavender growing, then I hear His whisper. That is one reason I think I love spring so much.

I remember my first lesson on weeding a garden as a young girl outside with my grandfather. I had the best grandpa. He was loving and kind and stern when needed. There I was, standing in front of my grandparent's big beautiful garden stretched out before my eyes. He pointed out a weed and told me to pull it, so I reached down and pulled and pulled and it broke off even with the dirt. I figured I had done well, after all it was not really visible anymore. He looked over at my work and bent down and pulled up the root and all, and said, "it's okay you aren't strong enough yet." I went on about my happy way, never to think of it again until years later when gardening with my husband.

Early in our marriage, I was helping my husband garden (and by helping, I mean basically watching, because that man can grow anything and watching him tend to a garden with such gentle peace and the Father's heart is one of my most favorite things in this life). He was pulling weeds, and I bent down to grab one and broke it right off at the dirt. I went on to the next one like nothing, when he asked me what I was doing. He asked me why I didn't pull up the whole root. He then told me how it will keep coming back over and over and even spread if I don't remove the root. I looked at him like he was crazy and then I said it, a phrase I realize at this moment that I overused throughout most of my life, "I am just not strong enough." He looked at me lovingly and pointed to the garden tool he had laid beside me and said, "Why don't you use the tool I gave you?"

Pause and let that sink in a second! Because I stood there frozen in time.

Wow… How much truth is in that one statement? Let's use the tools of the kingdom, the tools our heavenly Father so freely gives us to destroy and remove (permanently) whatever root the enemy has planted to lie to us, trick us, and keep us in bondage.

What has he planted in your life? Fear? Unforgiveness? Bitterness? Unworthiness? Regret? Pain? Disease? Lust? Depression? Anger? Confusion? Insecurity? Whatever it is, it only takes one time! Today, let's use the tool of prayer to pull up those weeds and to regularly do a heart check to see what lies we have allowed to trespass and take root in our hearts and minds!

Pray with me:

Father, we come to You with thankfulness for the tools you have given to us to change our lives, and the lives of others around us, in Your holy name! Right now, Lord, we pull that _____ root out, toss it in the fire, and move on, because Your Word says, "It is finished." In Jesus' name we pray, AMEN!

Next, spend some time jotting down some "roots" you feel need uprooted once and for all. Ask yourself, and answer truthfully, have you have used the tools God makes available? Maybe you didn't know you had tools, or how to even use them. That's okay, start today.

3

When you aren't strong enough on your own

But He said to me "My grace us sufficient for you, for My power is made perfect in weakness."
2 Corinthians 12:9

Back to weeding our garden.

The beauty of the Lord brings to my remembrance those two moments in time. When I was a child, my grandpa knew I was not yet strong enough, nor understood how to wield a garden tool. So, he did it for me. Later, when I was more mature, and physically strong enough, my husband told me how to do it using the tool. Both moments, both lessons right from the Father's heart. There are times when we aren't strong or wise enough.

In those places, God will sovereignly move on our behalf. He loves us that much. Other times, when we have the wisdom and strength, He doesn't leave us, but tells us how to do it and also partners with us to make it work. Sometimes, the hardest thing to do is admit we aren't strong enough on our own. Realizing and admitting that allows God's power to move miraculously. So, when we look back, or other people see it, there becomes no other explanation but God! He is real, and He is good.

But here I want to point out a weed we allow to stay often. We can use weakness as a way to get out of doing anything. We have a choice to make. Do we want to pull the root so it can no longer hinder our growth? Or do we just keep breaking it off and being surprised when it pops back up?

In Exodus 4:10-15. Moses says, "Lord, use someone else. I am just not good at this." God says, "No, I know you aren't good at it. Go anyway. I will be with you!"

Why do we even try and tell God what we are or aren't? He created us. He knows our heart better than we do. He did not allow Moses to bow out because of his weakness. Because He knew the strength was His own and the plan would not fail. He also knew what Moses was created to do. The same applies to you and me.

Ask yourself, what you have bowed out of because of your own fear or weaknesses? Submit those to God. Pray and ask God to show you how He wants to show His strength in those weak, doubtful areas in your life.

Earlier, you read a physical example of me not being strong enough to pull weeds out by the root. You see, I learned I was allowing spiritual weeds to remain in my heart as well. Meanwhile, God was waiting patiently to show me the tools He had given me access to, in order to pull the weeds up once and for all. He wants to help you, too. You just have to believe.

4

only ONE root

*When He saw they had finished breakfast, Jesus said to
Simon Peter, "Simon, son of Jonah, do you love Me?
He said to him, "Yes Lord, you know that I love you."
Jesus said to him, "Feed my lambs."
John 21:15-25*

*But the fruit of the Spirit is love, joy, peace, forbearance,
kindness, goodness, faithfulness, gentleness and self-control.
Against such things there is no law."
Galatians 5:22-23*

Today I want us to see the importance of only ONE
root... Love! Be rooted in Jesus so that all the fruit in your
life is from love.

I love the above scripture in the gospel of John. If
you read it all, you will see not once, but three times
JESUS asks Simon Peter if he loves Him. Every time the
answer is, "Yes, of course Lord. You know I love YOU!"

How many of you know God doesn't ask a question because He doesn't know the answer? He already knows every answer, and what is in our heart. He asks us so we become aware of it ourselves.

But what happens next always blows me away. Jesus tells him three times that, "if you love Me, do my work, do what I say." He is saying, hey how about you show that love you confess with some action?

Friends, love requires action, and that action looks different for each of us. I am not talking about one action here and there when you feel like it, either. I am talking about a laid down, surrendered life right where you are, right now, that is full of action. (By the way, rest is also an action). If you are truly rooted in Christ, it will flow out of you freely just by living your day-to-day life (read and pray Ephesians 3:14-21). If He is the only root in your heart, and you truly believe He is who He says He is, you will live a life of radical obedience and love easily.

The beauty here is it will look different for you and for me, because we are different parts of the same body working together. The fruit will be the same, and the Word says they (the world) will know us by our fruit! He tells Peter three times, "If you love Me you will: feed my lambs, tend my sheep, feed my sheep." Then later He says, "follow Me, do what I do, do what I say." And it's not the first time He had to tell the disciples this. He tells them and shows them more than once. Just like He does us.

He is good like that.

He doesn't say: "Well, okay, only feed, tend, and love the sheep that are cute and clean, or smell good, or are easy to handle, or are only the ones from your own backyard." No, He commands us (if we really love Him, that is) to feed and tend and love them all.

Pray with me:

Lord, we pray from right where we are. Even if we are still digging up and pulling out the weeds of lies, and even if we are just learning to water that one root of love with your truth and Word. Lord, we choose to believe You are who You say You are. We choose to be rooted only in Your love, Lord. We choose to walk that love out today, not just talk about it. Because WE DO love You Lord, we will do as you command us, even when it isn't comfortable or easy. In Your Holy name we pray, AMEN.

NOW GO! He is calling you to follow Him!

But the fruit of the Spirit

is love, joy, peace, patience,

kindness, goodness,

faithfulness, gentleness,

and self-control.

Against such things there

is no law."

Galatians 5:22-23

NIV

5

Every fruit is first a flower

*"Then God said, "Let the land produce vegetation:
seedbearing plants and trees on the land that bear fruit with
seed in it, according to their various kinds." And it was so.
The land produced vegetation: plants bearing seed according
to their kinds and trees bearing fruit with seed in it according
to their kinds. And God saw that it was good. And there was
evening, and there was morning the third day."*
Genesis 1:11-13

Every fruit is first a seed, then a bloom.

When you find yourself in a blooming season, then position yourself for kingdom ideas, revelation, and plans to be downloaded. Just like a blooming flower awaits fertilization before it can bear fruit, the same holds true for you and me, metaphorically. The flower blooming is the promise that fruit is on the way!

The Holy Spirit of God overshadows us when we are in blooming seasons, and those moments are where we start to produce fruit. That's why I say blooming is for the world, too. Growth, root development, and even pruning is often for our personal growth. But the blooming, it captivates those around us. It's beautiful, and most know blooming comes after hidden seasons. And ultimately, if we wait, those blooms will one day be fruit. Fruit those around you can eat of.

When you find yourself in a blooming season, you have to be mindful to not allow the flowers to be clipped off. Sometimes, even well-meaning people around us are so captivated by the bloom, by the promise and plans they see in this early stage, that they can convince you to clip the flowers and put them on display. Sometimes, we do it to ourselves, too. But when the flower is clipped from the vine, it starts to die. Nothing can grow apart from the vine. And blooms are not what sustain, the fruit is. The blooming stage is a beautiful promise of what is to come, but we are not "known" by how well we bloom. We are known by the fruit. Your character and conduct in the blooming seasons will help produce fruit. But ultimately, it's a product of abiding in Christ. It is the Holy Spirit that produces the fruit.

Spend some time today praying and asking God what fruit He wants you to grow, and what area you may be inhibiting growth. Keep track of divine ideas and plans you feel like are from the Lord.

Remember, God's timing is always good.

6

Faith sometimes means, letting go

"So neither the one who plants nor the one who waters is anything, but only God, who makes things grow."
1 Corinthians 3:7

I remember when my children were little, they were always wanting to plant any seed they found.

"Is this a seed, momma? Let's plant it and
see what grows!"

Their little hands would dig in the soil and plug in whatever they thought was a seed. Or, we would place the seed in a little cup of dirt, or clay flower pot. Not all seeds grew, but some did. And we learned together the truth: that we were made to partner with creation and also enjoy it. Jesus uses many metaphors and parables about seeds in the gospels. There are life lessons we can learn if we sit in the garden, or, better yet, walk with the gardener regularly.

I remember one particular season, my oldest son was so deeply grieved over the abundance of acorns in our yard. He saw they had the potential, but would not ever become mighty oak trees. I sat down one evening to research oak trees better to help him understand. In those moments, I realized many things about my son's heart, oak trees, and God. I wish I could tell you that at that time I saw the connection between who my son was becoming, and how his love for making things grow was actually taken right from the image of our Heavenly Father. But I did not understand that completely yet. It would be years later, after a particular tragedy, that I would make the correlation. He is a natural leader. He encourages with words, and actions. He tells the truth always, and if he sees your God-given potential, he tries to help create an environment for growth.

But only God can make things grow.

That was what my son had to learn. He can't control the actual growth, no matter how much work he puts in. It's a hard lesson. One that maybe you have been faced with, too. We can plant seeds, but ultimately, we can't make them grow. Even if we really want them to. Also, realize it's not about what I can do on my own, anyway.

It is actually freeing when we realize God is who makes things grow. So if I do my part, a good seed is always worth sowing. I water it with love and pull weeds when needed. But I am also okay with letting go and having faith that God is who gives the increase and growth is for His glory (1 Corinthians 3).

Did you know oak trees aren't made to grow in front yards? Not really. They are made to grow in the forest. Yet, they grow in many front yards, and they give shade and sturdy branches for a good rope swing, too.

We don't always get to decide what grows where. But regardless, there is always purpose.

Is there anything you need to let go?

Pray with me:

Lord, right now we place ___ in Your more than capable hands, and we have faith You will make it grow when and where it's needed. We ask that You give us strength to let go, and to help any unbelief in our hearts that may be standing in the way. Your Word says You will finish every good work You start. We receive that promise in Jesus' name, amen.

"Where flowers bloom, so does hope."

- Lady Bird Johnson

Peony Facts

- Once planted they can bloom for over 100 years.

- The peony has been around since 1000 BC.

- When Marco Polo saw the flower for the first time in Asia, he described them as "roses as big as cabbages," probably because some varieties can be up to 10 inches in diameter.

- They grow native in Asia, Europe, and North America, but they do prefer a colder winter, so here in America they are often considered a "northern flower."

- They come in almost every color except blue. Red is the rarest.

- They don't change colors, but their seeds can. So don't be surprised if you plant a white one, and years later some pink or yellow grows around it.

- Peonies are the Indiana state flower.

Things I've learned from growing peonies for over almost 20 years:

- ❀ Plant them in the fall. The colder weather will help them get established.

- ❀ Fertilize them in the spring.

- ❀ They like well-draining soil, and a lot of sun.

- ❀ Water them every other day in the hottest part of summer.

- ❀ Remember to be patient when planting a new plant. They are slow starters, and most do not bloom till the 3rd year.

7

Bloom strong

Bloom: (verb) a beautiful process of becoming.

*"Every branch in Me that does not bear fruit, He takes away;
and every branch that bears fruit, He prunes it so that it may
bear more fruit."*
John 15:2

*"Why, you do not even know what will happen tomorrow.
What is your life? You are a mist that appears for a little
while and then vanishes."*
James 4:14

Every year, I am so happy when my peonies bloom.
But one day, while I was clipping them off before the
forecasted chance of rain, I thought about life and how
fleeting it is. The peony blooms once in the spring; that's
it. Granted, each plant can produce multiple blooms that

last 7-10 days. It fills the air with fragrance so heavenly and makes the spring bridal bouquet breathtaking.

Then it's over.

Just like that, nature teaches us that we can be blooming today and not tomorrow. But what those blooms do while they are blooming is what's important. What they share and bring to the atmosphere is what matters. I recently read how to make your peonies produce a more productive, beautiful blooming season. It said to go out and strip all the smaller buds off the stems. That will focus the plants' energy on the strongest, biggest buds and make them more successful and fruitful. Similar to why we prune fruit trees.

In that moment, I realized all the things I personally say yes to, the things that are good and helpful and even appear to be beautiful, but are not really fruitful or what I should be focusing on. The things that help someone for a minute, and do nothing good for them in the long run. As for myself, I want to bloom to full capacity with what the Lord calls me to. I want that for you, too. I want the flowers (and fruit) to be so spectacular, that it draws others in just to see and smell and feel how beautiful God's glory is. This is in sincere hope that it inspires them to go out and bloom just as beautifully because it is not a competition.

You can have a bunch of smaller blooms that weigh the stalk down with droopy heads that break in the first rain of the season. Or you can have a huge, full bloom that stands strong in the wind and rain. One that stretches for the sun and feeds the bees and hummingbirds because she knows what she is doing today is what matters, and she knows her life is a mist that appears for just a little while.

Pray with me:

Lord, we thank You that there is enough time to do all the things YOU have called us to do. We pray that You uncover and remove any unproductive buds that will only weigh us down in this life. And that we bloom so strong and beautiful for Your glory while we are here, Lord, because we know this worldly life is a vapor, here today and gone tomorrow. But the life You give us is eternal and we thank You for that! In Jesus' name we pray, amen.

Now, spend some time jotting down any places you feel may need pruned off. Ask the Holy Spirit to help you. Maybe things that look good at first glance, and even have potential to produce small, weak blooms. Make a list of things you know God has asked you to do with your one life. If you can't, ask Him to speak now. Then, pay attention to things you love, have passion for, and can't get off your mind or heart. There is no shame here. But the goal is to grow strong and bloom for a purpose.

8

I am who You say I am

In our culture, you can see the interest in identity everywhere. We see personality quizzes, books, and a never-ending search to know who we really are. This is also a doorway that the enemy can often slip in and bring labels and alternatives to the truth. Often, those feel "good" at first or even harmless. But over time, you still feel like something is missing, and the search doesn't end... ever.

That's one reason (out of many) that it's so important to know your identity in Christ. Everything stems from that knowing. When we start living from a place of being a son/daughter of God instead of orphan, servant, or slave... everything changes. The way we look at the world around us changes, not just how we look in the mirror.

We were made in God's image, and in Genesis chapter 1, (let's start at the beginning, creation) you'll read that we are the only thing creation God called "very good" (verse 31).

We were made to be set apart. We are predestined for adoption as it says in Ephesians 1:5. You aren't a mistake or accident.

But today, I'm going to start with who God is and talk about who we are in the next devotion. Because we can't understand who we are until we know who our Creator is. We can't reflect His attributes to the world around us if we don't know them.

There are many names and titles for God scattered all throughout scripture, and each one shows us a different part of His character. El Shaddai (which means God Almighty) will tell you a different story than El Roi (the God who sees me).

Abba (Father)
Everlasting Father
Alpha and Omega, the first and the last, the beginning and the end The Great Physician
Healer
Wonderful Counselor
The Good Shepherd
Immanuel (God with us)

That's not even close to all of them, and each one holds more insight than one can imagine.

Studying these names of God helped me a lot. It helped transform me from 'orphan' to 'daughter.' From 'servant' to 'friend.' And it can for you as well.

If you don't know who God is, and what the Word of God says, you don't know what He isn't, either. So, it will be harder to see the fake that the enemy throws at us. Only by knowing the truth, can you tell when a lie comes in. It's key to an overall healthy heart, and to running the glorious race set before you.

You were created for God, by God.

You have a purpose.

You are loved more than you can fathom.

God wants to and can fill every place in your mind, body, and soul that is crying out for something, anything, to feel complete and whole. And to answer the deep question, "who am I?"

Just remember, you can't know or love yourself or anyone else until you know and love who God is. You have to have knowledge of both who God really is and who God says you are. You won't get it all today, or this week even. The facets of God are many, and truth and knowledge are never ending. But keep asking, and keep listening. I promise, He won't leave or forsake you (Deuteronomy 31:6).

Take some time to write down some lies you've believed, and then also replace them with truth.

To the one who feels unseen, unappreciated, or unheard:

It's ok, because the only One who matters sees you, He appreciates you, and He hears you!

In this world, sometimes we confuse accountability, encouragement, and testifying with plain old bragging. I've done it. I've done something well and wanted someone/anyone to be proud of me. To show me "honor," only to learn that kind of honor is shallow. It is fake. I have come to learn that real Godly honor, and friendship, will open doors in Heaven. But flattery? It's just another form of gossip and I don't want it. Neither should you. If He says don't do it, don't do it. Don't ask why, just don't do it.

Check your heart today, and if you're feeling hurt or let down by people, or like you have to work to prove something to those around you, stop. Remember, when you live for Jesus, you don't need anyone else's approval.

Pray with me:

Lord, we come to You with empty hands today, because only empty hands can be open hands able to be filled! We thank You for loving us and equipping us to grow closer to being more like You daily. Give us strength, Lord, in this media-driven, fast paced world, to look up more than we look around or down. In Jesus' name we pray, amen.

9

No comparison

"Each one should test their own actions.
Then they can take pride in themselves alone, without
comparing themselves to someone else."
Galatians 6:4

Many of us struggle with an unhealthy habit of comparing ourselves to others. Comparing what we have, how we look, our gifts and talents, and the seasons of life we are currently in. First of all, let me warn you: comparison will leave a legacy of unhappiness... every single time. Second, comparison gives birth to insecurity and strife. This is the enemy's number one way to divide and thwart God's plans. It makes us abort our missions without even realizing we are doing it, and it plants nasty roots that spread.

One day while clipping roses, I had two roses in my hand and a thorn pricked me. Both were equally beautiful, yet different. Color, petals, foliage, fragrance, and the number of thorns on one were a few noticeable differences.

But as the gardener, I loved them equally. As the gardener, I don't love the red rose less because of her thorns. I handle her with more gentle care and grace.

That is God's heart for each of us. He sees our differences and even our flaws and He loves us equally. The red rose appeals to one and the yellow another, uniquely created differently for a purpose.

Here is the truth: when you compare yourself to another, you're acting in disobedience to God. That may sound tough, but it needs to be said.

Stop doing it.

You are where you are and have the gifts and talents and personality traits you have for a reason. Embrace what is good, work on what is not good, and choose to find contentment in Christ.

Pray with me:

Lord, right now I come to You with a thankful heart that You call me fearfully and wonderfully made. I embrace the unique traits You have given me. You know me by name, and I am important to and loved by You. I repent for any time I have compared myself or my seasons to others, and I ask that you fill those surrendered places in my heart right now with peace and love and contentment that only You can give! In Jesus' name I pray, amen.

10

"The grass wither, the flowers fade, but the Word of our God stands forever."

Isaiah 40:8

I will never forget the way her brown eyes would twinkle when she smiled. There was a language barrier, but that didn't matter. It was my first time in her nation of Nicaragua, and I had never felt so welcome anywhere. We were on a mission trip, distributing and setting up water filters in the countryside. We walked from house to house, and at first the thought felt "scary" for lack of a better word. You hear so many opinions about being safe, that if we aren't careful, we will forget Jesus never told us to "be safe". This life is anything but safe and comfortable. It's so much better.

We walked up in their yard, and Estrella was on the porch playing. She immediately smiled. Her grandma came out, and invited us in. I stayed on the porch with her. I would occasionally steal the interpreter to have him find out her name and what she was trying to say to me. We realized she wanted to touch my hair.

There we sat, total opposites. Her dark skin, dark hair, and dark eyes. My light skin, light hair, and light eyes. I quickly realized she may have never seen anyone like me in her short 6 years in this rural part of her third world nation.

The others were busy doing the water filter stuff. But I sat with her while she studied me. How alike we really were, yet different. I told her Jesus loved her in my best Spanish. Which made her laugh. But she nodded like she knew Him already, and loved Him, too. We were about to leave when she grasped my hand and tugged. I bent down and she hugged me. It took all my strength not to weep. Not to stay. Not to try and do something, anything, more practical to change her life. Then the peace that surpasses all understanding washed over me, and I knew God was there. He would not leave or forget her any more than he would my own daughter. He had a good plan for Estrella.

Estrella means star, her grandma told us. It is also a variation of the name Esther.

We made it back down to the dirt road to continue on, when we heard the little Nicaraguan Esther calling to me as she ran alongside the hill with the hand-woven wire fence. I walked over to meet her, and she stretched her little arm across the wire, and I stretched mine. She handed me a tiny white flower. She smiled, waved, and ran back to her grandma who was calling her name.

I stood there. This tiny white clover-like flower in my hand. I looked at it and wanted to preserve the beauty of the moment forever. I tucked it in the little leather travel bible I had in my hand and walked on.

I will probably never see Estrella earth-side again, or most of the people we met on that trip, or the others I've met when I've been on trips since. But I am assured I will see her in heaven one day. Her picture is on my refrigerator like my own children, nieces, and nephews.

And that flower is dried in between the pages of John 3:16. It stays as a reminder to my own heart when it feels hopeless at the world around me. For God so loved the WHOLE world, not just a few places, but the whole world!

For centuries, people have been pressing and drying flowers and botanicals in between pages of books to preserve them. It's not new. The yearning to preserve beauty and moments is hardwired in our human nature. God created the earth for us to enjoy and care for. He wants us to slow down and look at the beauty in creation, and to appreciate it. But the Word of God is the most spectacular gift He has given us. It is packed full of instruction and promises about how He loves and cares for us.

The earth will fade away, but God's word never fails or fades away. He is faithful.

Pray and ask The Holy Spirit to help you:

Record any moment in your life you wished you could preserve and save the beauty of. Also, think about the moments you knew that God helped you, encouraged you, and saved you. (Remember, God is in everything, even the broken moments. If He reveals something broken to you, He wants to heal it.)

To plant a garden is to believe in

tomorrow.

-Audrey Hepburn

How to Preserve & Dry Flowers

There are many ways to preserve and dry botanicals, but here are two of my favorite ways.

Book press method:

You'll need…

- Fresh flowers (or leaves, or whatever botanical you want to preserve)

- A heavy book

- Parchment paper (for best results) to help protect the pages of the book or an absorbent paper (like a paper towel)

Instructions…

- Arrange flower(s) on parchment paper, and place another sheet of paper on top.

- Close the book and set a heavy object on top to help apply pressure.

- Wait 2-4 weeks for the flower to completely dry.

DIY Wooden Press Method:

(You can find store-bought wooden flower presses if you don't want to make your own.)

What you'll need...

- 2 12"x12" pieces of plywood/mdf or oak shelving board

- Cardboard (two pieces cut to fit the above wood shape)

- Parchment or blotting paper

- 4 bolts and wingnuts (and basic knowledge of how to use a drill)

Instructions...
- Drill four holes in the corners of the wood you chose.

- Arrange flower(s) between two pieces of parchment paper, and then two pieces of cardboard.

- Sandwich the pressed flowers between the two pieces of wood. Then, tighten the bolts and nuts through the holes in each corner.

- Wait 2-4 weeks for the flower to completely dry.

A Prayer

Today, I pray you sit at His feet for a while and thank Him for the blessings all around you. Ask Him to show you. Ask Him to lead you in His Word to His promises. Ask Him to speak to you. Then listen.

I pray you look around you at the beauty unfolding. I pray that you see the promise of the harvest that is coming, and you are eager to join in. Because He needs workers. He needs gatherers. He needs lovers. He needs weed-pullers and waterers and teachers to sow the seeds for the next generation. What part will you play? Friend, you don't want to miss what's up ahead. My "what next, what now, what if" answers may look different than yours. But rest assured, they are not any less important.

"Then He (Jesus) said to his disciples, The harvest is plentiful, but the laborers are few; therefore, pray earnestly to the Lord of the harvest to send out laborers into his harvest."
Matthew 9:37-38

11

Be intentional in your pursuit

"You will seek Me and you will find Me, when you seek Me with all your heart."
Jeremiah 29:13

My mother got me this beautiful butterfly field guide and a butterfly feeder for my birthday one year. One day soon after, I was sitting minding my own business in the garden. I was trying to identify this little butterfly fettering around, and it flew over and landed on my finger, lingering for a while. That had never happened to me before, just like I'd never noticed the mockingbird on the fence post in the early morning. Now I see it every day. Coincidence?

No.

Another example is when my son turned 16 years old, he drove a dark green Toyota. At one time, I lost count how many dark green Toyotas I saw locally. But they were always there. It was an older car. I just never really looked, before I had a reason to.

When you search for something, you will find it.

When you choose to stop and look around you, you will see so much in life that was always there, but you never noticed. That's like listening to God. I hear people say they don't hear Him speak. Well, have you ever really listened? Because the moment you put as much intention into listening to and abiding with Jesus as we do our tv's, phones, or our friends, I promise- you'll hear Him.

Pray with me:

Lord, I ask You to help me uncover what I am really seeking. Whatever I may be looking at too long, any voice I am listening to that does not line up with Yours, reveal it. I want to seek You, Lord, with my whole heart. I want to hear Your voice above all others around me. Thank You, Lord, that Your Word promises that when I seek You, I will find You. In Jesus' name, amen.

"May the God of hope fill you with joy and peace as you trust in Him, so that you may overflow with hope by the power of the Holy Spirit."
Romans 15:13

Now, use this space to write. Ask yourself these questions and write down honestly what comes to mind.

❀ What am I searching for?

❀ How do those things line up with God's Word?

_____

_____

_____

_____

_____

_____

_____

❀ How do those things line up with an abundant
   life?

_____

_____

_____

_____

_____

_____

_____

_____

_____

_____

_____

❀ Are the music, media, books, and magazines I am taking in, giving life?

_____

_____

_____

_____

_____

_____

_____

_____

❀ The food I eat, does it give life?

_____

_____

_____

_____

_____

_____

_____

_____

_____

_____

_____

❋ My relationships- are they giving life? If the answer is no, ask Holy Spirit to reveal how you can bring life into the relationship. It's not all one sided, so remember that.

We know scripture tells us our words can either carry
life or death (Proverbs 18:21).

❀ Are the words I'm speaking giving life?

Declare this over yourself:

My words are powerful. They can help, heal, and encourage, or they can wound, hinder, or humiliate. I choose to use life-giving words when I talk to others and about myself.

"Sin is not ended by multiplying words,
but the prudent hold their tongues."
Proverbs 10:19

"Do not let any unwholesome talk come out of your mouths,
but only what is helpful for building others up according to
their needs, that it may benefit those who listen."
Ephesians 4:29

"But I tell you that everyone will have to give account on the
day of judgment for every empty word they have spoken.
For by your words you will be acquitted, and by
your words you will be condemned."
Matthew 12:36-37

Facts about Poppies

The **anemone** or **poppy** are the "wild lilies" that are traditionally identified as 'Lily of the Field.'

Around Jerusalem, the red shade is more frequent while on the slopes of the sea of Galilee, while the hillside is speckled with blue and white flowers.

These are wild field flowers in and around Israel, and they almost certainly are the wild anemones that were referred to by Jesus as the 'lilies of the field' in His sermon on the mount. They still grow wild near the Lake of Galilee today.

"Consider the lilies of field, and how they grow"
(taken from Matt 6:28-30)

In Hebrew, the flower is called Kalanit- which is from Kala or "bride." And in the Greek, it means "wind."

12

Thou the mountain may crumble,
You will not.
Isaiah 54:10

Keep reading in Isaiah 54, and He says, "and the hills be removed, yet my unfailing love for you will not be shaken nor my covenant of peace be removed," says the Lord, who has compassion on you.

Sometimes, if you're like me, we take our eyes off our Creator. We take our eyes (even if it is only for a moment) off the Only One with the real answers. Because we think we can do it quicker maybe, or better even, or that it's not that important to God because "there are bigger things going on in the world." Those are all lies. Nothing is too small or too big for God. There is no worldly answer or any other way to fix anything. He is the only way, the only truth, the only light. Abide in His peace and remember it's a covenant that cannot be broken! Because even though we are often a covenantbreaking, unfaithful people, He is not!

What if I told you grief and trauma aren't the same thing? What if I told you that it's the enemy of our soul that reminds us of trauma, and it's not actually part of healthy, holy grief?

One morning, God gave me a vision of a bridge. He said, "My church/body is divided amongst themselves." On one side some were sitting, wringing their hands with frustration over this world and waiting for His return. The other side was running rescue missions to heal the sick, raise the dead, and cast out demons in Jesus' name while waiting for His return. But both sides were arguing over who was right. Both sides were wasting so much time with each other, while the lost were still lost, the sick were still sick, and the demons were still running wild seeking whom they may devour. However, this is not always the case, and there is fruit on both sides. He walks among both sides, too. But, you guys, He is calling every part of His body to do what they are designed to do. The foot can't do the eye's part.

One day, soon after this vision, I ran into a man who most people don't even look at (other than to judge or talk about his past and what he could have or should have done). I walked by and honestly, that day I wasn't even looking at him either. But he called out to me. He thought I was someone else in my family. He thought I was my aunt, then my sister, and asked if I was "better." I told him I wasn't her, and she was better but had passed away. His eyes filled up. He had just lost a sibling, also.

Tears started to run down his face. And right there I saw his eyes, sober, clean, and clear. And I saw Jesus in there... in a "washed up old addict."

The look on his face stayed on my heart for days, and it still brings me to tears. I didn't have a bunch of words bubble up or scriptures to offer. I just hugged him. I wrapped my arms around him. In our suffering, we were the same. I told him I was thankful for him, and I saw the actual shock in his eyes. The unworthiness and lies of the enemy were all over his face. But then I saw the belief wash over his face, and he said thank you. And Jesus was right there with us.

Suffering is a topic I think is overlooked often and ignored even at times. But suffering is where I've seen Jesus the most. He really is strongest when we are weakest.

Love is the bridge.
Love is the answer.

LOVE IS ACTION!
Therefore go!
(Matthew 28:19)

13

Brave Surrender

What stumps many Christians, is that often God won't use you in the way you want to be used. Are you willing to do what He says anyway? Really?

Being committed is about what we can do ourselves. But being surrendered, whew... that's being willing to let God do what only He can do and being okay with whatever that looks like. No, okay isn't the right word. It's about being *joyful* no matter what it looks like.

Are you committed, or are you surrendered?

A lot of good can come out of commitment. It is a great character trait that we should all strive for. But miracles, signs, and wonders come from being surrendered, too.

Honestly, it's easier to commit. Because we can work for God. Most are good at that. Because it is usually predictable. But surrender means I don't work for Him; I work with Him. I abide in Him. I believe in His promises. Jesus didn't say to go and do things to be salt and light.

He said YOU are salt and light, because of Him, and what He did. Nothing I can do myself. I just have to believe, and from that moment, that whether I've read the whole bible or only John 3:16 on the back of semi-truck, I am salt and light.

"You are the salt of the earth"

"You are the light of the world"

(taken from Matthew 5:13-16)

From this place of understanding comes a surrendered life. It's everyday life, not only on Sunday, or at conferences, or on social media live videos. It's how we live day in and day out. It's a heart posture of resting in the truth that God loves me no matter what I can or can't do for Him. No matter what I do or don't do for Him.

My life can either make people taste and see that the Lord is good, or it can poison and blind them. One way or another, if you are walking around on this earth, your life is preaching some kind of message.

So, are you surrendered or committed?

Read that again. I'm not championing disobedience here (the opposite actually). Surrender means joyful obedience!

Those who are committed often achieve a lot quickly: awards, recognition, and applause of man. But those who are surrendered make history. Their character may not be revealed until the end. But their treasures are in heaven and the seeds are eternal. But the truth is, it is easier to commit to serving Jesus than it often is to truly follow Him (surrender).

Today, I challenge you to surrender. Moses chose to surrender and was used to set captives free! Jesus chose to surrender. His life was not taken from Him. He gave it freely. Because of that, we are free as well, and we hold the power to help set others free, too.

Will you?

To the "late bloomer"

"And we know that in all things God works for the good of those who love him, who have been called according to his purpose."
Romans 8:28

I hear the Lord saying, "I AM never late. What the world calls late I call on time. I call for such a time as this."

Maybe you needed to be moved. Maybe your soil needed to be amended. Or maybe that big storm stunted your growth or broke your stems. Or maybe everything was always okay and part of the plan, but you just looked around at everyone else blooming and figured you missed it somewhere, somehow, or were forgotten.

But today God is saying, "Nothing I plant is ever late. Every promise and plan will come to pass. You will bloom."

Remember…

"You were born for such a time as this"
Esther 4:14

Lavender Lemonade

A refreshing spin on the classic

summer drink. Make a batch,

chill, and enjoy on a warm day.

Feel free to experiment, and tweak

the sweetener to your liking.

Ingredients:

- 1 cup freshly squeezed lemon juice (I prefer Meyer lemons)

- 4 cups water, divided

- 1 cup honey (or sugar or sweetener of choice)

- 1 tablespoon dried or fresh from the garden lavender flowers

- Ice

- Lemon slices and lavender sprigs for garnish

Instructions:

- Add 2 cups of water, the honey, and the dried lavender to a small pot. Bring to a simmer over medium heat and stir to dissolve the honey.

- Once the honey is dissolved, turn off the heat and let the mixture infuse for 30 minutes.

- While you're waiting for the mixture to infuse, pour the lemon juice into a pitcher.

- Strain the lavender mixture through a fine mesh strainer into the pitcher with the lemon juice.

✤ Pour 2 cups of cold water (or more, if desired) into the pitcher and stir together.

✤ Add ice and lemon slices.

To serve, pour the lemonade in glasses over ice, and garnish with a lemon slice and lavender sprig if desired. Enjoy!

14

Where did the flowers go?

"One day you will look back and see all along you were blooming."
Morgan Harper Nichols

It was so hot that summer day, and some parts are kind of a blur, even now, seven years later. Have you ever found yourself in a story you don't want to be in, or even know how you can survive it? We all have on some level, I am sure. That's where I was. If you had asked me then, I would have said I was not sure what was blooming well, or blooming at all. My younger sister was sick. She had been diagnosed just the summer before. Looking back from here, I see all the growth and blooming that was there all along. And even if the story isn't one I would have chosen, I regret nothing.

One particularly hot Florida day, someone came by the house and brought some flowers (a mixture of roses and sunflowers and some filler). I made a mental note that it was something my sister would have picked. The sweet friend went on to visit with my sister, and I went on cooking dinner. My brother-in-law would be home from work soon, and then off to take the littlest boy to baseball practice. I remember placing the flowers in a vase of water, setting them aside, and moving on.

I personally think grief in the midst of life may be the hardest thing I have ever been through. Most think it's the grief you have after death, which is a different kind of hard. But death is final. It can't be argued. If you are a believer, we know it's only temporarily final, for us left here on earth. But the promise of eternal life awaits. What a glorious promise that is! But grief in the middle of life? Man… that is a battle. One, you have to give yourself daily to the Lord. He will strengthen you. You walk around wondering, "What next?" You mourn over your plans, the way you thought life would look, the way it "should be." It comes in many forms. Not just terminal illness, but divorce and other things can fit in there, too.

The day and evening went on, and something was off about the flowers. They looked funny. I could not put my finger on why. Something was missing. It wasn't the most important thing on my mind, so I went on. The next morning, I went in the boys' room to wake them up, and there on the nightstand between the boys' beds was a tall drinking glass filled with water, and some of the roses from the floral arrangement were just stuck in. They were not arranged or trimmed to fit the glass. Just sitting there. I walked across the short hall and there was one on their sister's bedside table, too.

I froze.

Her oldest son at the tender age of 11 woke first, from my initial entry. He started to get up, all flustered, not a morning person (he got that from his momma). He seemed more erratic than usual. I grabbed him and sat him down on the edge of the bed. The look in his big blue eyes (he got those from his momma, too) looked so sad, so heavy. That look is in my mind forever... the fear, anger, sadness.

I said, "Nice flowers. They really brighten the room," with a light laugh. He smiled, and what he said next changed the way I live my life. He said, "You said fresh flowers make you happy. That they change the attitude in the room. So, I was hoping it would do that for us, too."

I wondered when I had said that. It sounded like me. Then I realized he had been at our home in Illinois the month before for two weeks. He had watched me do day to day life. He must have watched me closely. We have no idea just how close we are being watched by those around us. Those who are thirsty for a drink of living water, and for a way out or through many things they are faced with.

I smiled and hugged him close, and asked him how that was going. He shrugged, and said, "Why do people clip them off the big plant? Don't they realize that kills them? They are dying right in front of us."

I sat there for a moment. I knew he was in deep thought. Then I reminded him and myself, too: we are all physically dying from the moment we are born. Whether it occurs at age 33 or 103. But what really matters is getting and staying connected to the eternal vine. From that place, we never die, not even when our flesh says otherwise (John 15).

I explained the gospel. I explained that we as branches must stay connected to the vine (Jesus) by abiding in Him. We don't have to perform or work to earn that connection. But we must choose to stay connected to the only true source of life.

Later that afternoon we went to the beach, and he asked to be baptized. So, his momma and I walked him out into the waves and prayed with him, and then and there he decided to follow Jesus. His eyes changed. They remained sad at times, but the fear was gone. He yelled, "Look, look, a rainbow!" We all smiled and cried a little, but we knew Heaven was rejoicing. God's peace was a promise; one He would not break. That simple sign would go on to be the biggest reoccurring one to this day for our family.

A rainbow. A promise.

Pray with me:

Lord, thank You that You loved us so we can love each other, with a love so fierce it conquers the grave. Because you live, so will I. In Your name we pray, amen.

Declare these words:

I will not die, BUT live and declare the works of the Lord.

If the grief you're feeling makes you feel hopeless, then take a break and journal these things out. And remember, Heaven is real and it's glorious. Ask Holy Spirit to guide you.

1. Write down how you really feel, raw and real.
2. Then remember this most important fact: God is not the author of confusion or sickness or disease (1 Corinthians 14:33). Jesus is the Prince of Peace. In Him, we have access to an abundant life.

Ask the Lord to replace what plans you feel you lost or that were stolen from you, with His hope and plans and promises. Write down what comes to mind.

"Here on earth you will have many trials and sorrows. But take heart, because I have overcome the world."

- Jesus

15

But I don't feel new!

"Therefore, if anyone is in Christ, he is a new creation. The old has passed away; behold, the new has come."
2 Corinthians 5:17

"What does it mean?" is what I get asked the most. To really understand the fullness of the new you, you have to look at the old. If you don't know the depth of what you were saved from, then grace and mercy don't mean much to you. Don't misunderstand me. Looking back is rarely a good thing. We should be looking at Jesus. But sometimes, He shows us a glimpse of what was, so we can fully see what is.

The law in the Old Testament was so layered, and impossible to fulfill. It brought an awareness of sin that created never ending shame and condemnation and a need for sacrifice and atonement.

But Jesus! The only way out! The grace of God brings an awareness of sin that makes me more aware of His goodness. It's simple: you become what you behold. Choose daily to behold Christ. Even if (or when) you stumble, His grace and mercy will gently pick you up and point you back to the right path... the narrow path.

From the minute we are filled with His Holy Spirit, we are eternally a brand-new creation, born again, forgiven, and a clean slate. But we are also still clay jars on the Potter's wheel. We still need molded and shaped (discipled) to look like the treasure we hold inside... to look like Jesus.

It is a process.

Many expect to wake up and all the consequences of our actions to be gone. That's not what it means. In heaven, they are gone. The Word says love keeps no record of wrongs and that God will remember our sins no more. We shouldn't, either.

It's true that right now, I am still a girl who had a baby at barely 18, got married young, divorced young, and made some mistakes in the middle. I've repented, been forgiven, and have had good, healthy relationships for years now. But my kids still go to two places on the holidays, and I still must deal with the consequences of my life choices. They don't disappear. This is where I see so many fall down and stay down, mad at God. Don't do that.

Ask Him, and He will show you how to live as a new creation now. Ask Him, and His Holy Spirit will guide you. It may look a bit different than someone who hasn't walked the same path as you. That's ok. God makes a way always. His Word has a solution for every problem.

Pray with me:

Lord, thank You for the way out. Thank You that Your blood makes all things new, even on days I don't feel it or see it. I take those feelings and thoughts captive right now, Lord. I give them to you, and I won't pick up those lies again. In Jesus' name, amen.

Spend some time praying and write down any areas you need to surrender. Write down any place you feel you are still struggling with in being a new creation. Think of any place you feel let down or even unsatisfied in your life.

God is big enough for our pain and our questions. He isn't mad at your feelings. But He does want you healed, healthy, and whole. Remember, unhealthy feelings will lie to you. We are called to walk by faith, not feelings. But God did give us feelings. So, aligning ours with His is the key.

16

Plant them anyway

"Go after a life of love as if your life depended on
it--- because it does"
1 Corinthians 14:1MSG

When I first married my husband, he promised me a rose garden. And boy, has he planted some roses, and many other flowers and trees. So many that he may regret that promise at times. Ha! He's not just planted them either, but tended to, watered, and fertilized. He can even be caught singing while he pulls weeds. He is a great example of our Father's heart for growing things. With a humble heart, he is like a walking encyclopedia; if you want to learn something, come for a visit. He has mastered the art of growing and blooming right where he is, in every season, no matter what. The first house we lived in together, we planted many roses believing we would never move again... ever! I would be a little old lady arranging flowers in my kitchen while my grandkids visited and ate homemade blueberry muffins at the table. That was my plan (emphasis on the word MY). And goodness this one rose, she was the most beautiful.

A Double Delight, she had long beautiful stems and dark green foliage, a creamy center with dark red tipped edges and the fragrance was perfect. But we moved, and she was so beautifully planted and well rooted I left her behind for the new owners.

Since living where I do now, in this big house in these little woods that I've grown to love, I've struggled to grow roses well. I've struggled to grow anything really, except weeds and what was already rooted and growing well when we moved in. Don't get me wrong, I have an immaculate flower garden due to the gardener before me, a lot of years of sweat and love, a little of my dreams, and a lot of my husband's TLC. So finally, after 7 years, we planted a new Double Delight.

Want to know the reason I waited years to plant one? Because I was waiting to move to the place I would live forever and love everything about. I was rushing ahead of the plan God had for my life. I couldn't stand the thought of planting another one and leaving her behind for someone to neglect or dig up like before. When I briefly think of the years I've wasted, years that I could have been admiring and enjoying this bloom, I could cry. But I won't. Because I know my God is the God of restoration and He knows the beginning and the end! And guess what? While I sit here and write this after 13 years packed full of so much life, God is moving us again. And again, I will leave Double Delight behind for the next owner.

My point is this: don't wait for what's next. Don't wait! Don't worry about your future feelings possibly being hurt. Grow and bloom, right now, right where you are! Even if you know it's not the final word, even if you are surrounded by trees and your heart is on the prairie, or the other way around. Grow and bloom anyway.

Keep only one root in your heart- Jesus! Everything else is meant to be pulled up and moved around. Don't waste time waiting around for perfection. Because it doesn't completely exist on this earth, anyway. We can have perfect memories, perfect sunrises, perfect sunsets, perfect kisses, perfect little moments carved out of time that may last for a minute but stay forever in our hearts, moments where heaven really touches earth. But ultimately, life is not meant to be perfect until we are finally home. God tells us to be awake and ready to go (Luke 12:35-48, Matthew 25: 1-13, and Thessalonians 5 to give a few examples). You can't be ready if you're rooted in this earth in one spot, and worried about what's next or not next. We need to be blooming and growing, and yet ready to pull up and go when He calls us. Leaving nothing behind except a beautiful legacy of God's love and truth, and maybe a few fragrant roses for the next one passing through.

So, take it from me, listen to the saying: "The true meaning of life is to plant trees whose shade you may never sit under." In this case, plant the roses you may never get to enjoy. Is worth it. Every single time.

What are some things you may be waiting on? Are you waiting for perfect conditions to do something God has told you to do? Or something you want to do? Take some time and pray, ask God to reveal any areas you may be waiting.

Pray with me:

Lord, help me uncover any areas in my life I have waited for too long a time. Forgive me. I thank You Lord that You are patient, and Your love never fails, even when I do. Thank you that you can restore and redeem anything, even time. Lord, help me to live life today, and to embrace the life you have for me. Help me to let go of any need for perfection. In Jesus' name, amen.

Spontaneous Bloom

"God's word is a seed."
Luke 8:11

Seeds I forgot I sowed

A little beauty tucked in the back of the garden.

unforeseen by many

But not unforeseen by the gardener

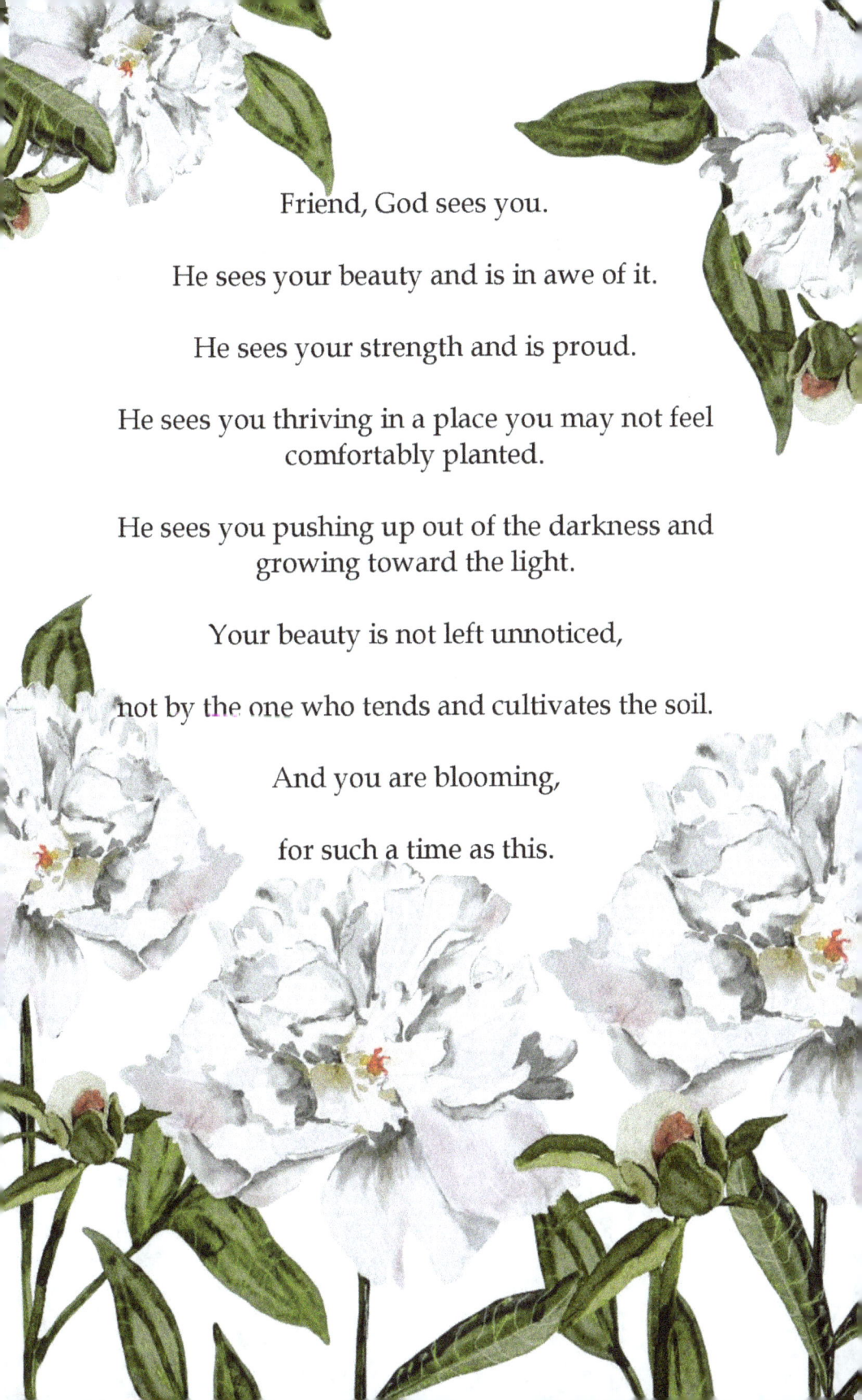

Friend, God sees you.

He sees your beauty and is in awe of it.

He sees your strength and is proud.

He sees you thriving in a place you may not feel
comfortably planted.

He sees you pushing up out of the darkness and
growing toward the light.

Your beauty is not left unnoticed,

not by the one who tends and cultivates the soil.

And you are blooming,

for such a time as this.

Rest today. Sometimes, less outside words are better. Lean in and listen to the sweet voice of the bridegroom calling His bride closer. Make a batch of lavender lemonade, or grab a cup of tea or coffee. Use this space to jot down anything you feel or sense, or spontaneous words you hear while praying and worshiping.

17

Don't fall for it, it's a trap

"The mystery that is, Christ in you, the hope of glory."
Colossians 1:24-29

Why is "the best version of me" trend a trap? One word: me. The best version of me can be found in the morning, after 2 cups of coffee and quiet. After watching the birds and reading what I want and clipping flowers from my garden. The best version of me can also be found on the beach once in a while. Nothing but sea air and laughter ringing in my ears.

But what about the days that aren't like those? Days of newborn babies, sick kids, kids late for school, baby goats in the bathtub because their mom died, broken eggs, running late to work in the mornings? I've woken up to tragedy that takes your breath away and stills the earth for a moment. I've watched death creep in slowly and take its time, too. In those moments, no one needed the best version of me. Not even myself. Because the very best version of me is still flawed and even weak at times. She can't save anyone on her own. She can't even if she tries, and she has tried. The world doesn't need the best version of me or you.

It needs Jesus.

It needs Jesus in you and in me.

The very best version of me (and you) can only be found in Him! I can do so much more from that truth. It's beautiful. It's freeing, too.

This world needs the strength and peace and salvation that can only come from a good God. It needs sons and daughters willing to lay down "what about me?" and pick up Him to really walk out their "best lives" on earth. Because this is not all there is. There is more! He wants you to come up higher and see the 'more.'

Also, never to stop romanticizing this blessing of life… the seasons, the good and the hard days. Because it is a gift, all of it, and He can use it all if you let Him.But I won't pretend it's because of anything I can do on my own, either.

Pray with me:

Lord, I thank You that You are strongest in my weakest moments. I do not have to work for Your love or salvation. Thank you for freeing me from me and from the lie that I can do everything on my own. Lord, help me to share Your light and love everywhere I go for Your glory. In Jesus' name, amen.

"Every good and perfect
gift is from above, coming down
from the Father of the heavenly lights,
who does not change like the shifting
shadows."

James 1:17

"Worship the Lord with gladness;
come before Him with joyful songs"
Psalm 100:2

I come to the garden alone,
While the dew is still on the roses;
And the voice I hear, falling on my ear,
The Son of God discloses.

And He walks with me, and He talks with me,
And He tells me I am His own,
And the joy we share as we tarry there,
None other has ever known.

He speaks, and the sound of His voice
Is so sweet the birds hush their singing;
And the melody that He gave to me
Within my heart is ringing

And He walks with me, and He talks with me,
And He tells me I am His own,
And the joy we share as we tarry there,
None other has ever known.

I'd stay in the garden with Him.

Hymn written by Charles Austin Miles USA 1868-1946. Born at Lakehurst, NJ, he attended the Philadelphia College of Pharmacy and the University of PA.

He became a pharmacist. He married Bertha H Haagen, and they had two sons: Charles and Russell. In 1892 he abandoned his pharmacy career and began writing gospel songs. At first, he furnished compositions to the Hall-Mack Publishing Company, but soon became editor and manager, where he worked for 37 years. He felt he was serving God better in the gospel song writing business, than as a pharmacist.

(Info Taken from hymnary.org)

18

Give Him your grief

"I come to the garden alone, while the dew is still on the roses."

"He heals the broken in heart, and binds up their wounds."
Psalm 147:3

I remember the first time I recognized healthy grief. Grief is such a taboo topic. It brings a lot of hidden feelings out in the open and the last thing you want to do is tell others how to do it.

I had grieved in my life, like all people. But I don't think I ever knew what to do, how to give it to God, and to really heal. I did it the way many do, with feelings, excuses, steps, or suppression. How the world says it should look. That's ok, until you realize there is a better way.

We were faced with an extreme amount of loss in a short time that spring. It would test everything I thought I knew about life, faith, and God. It was our first kidding season on our new goat farm adventure. It started with so much unexpected loss, and pain. Which anyone who has ever lived on a farm is familiar with. But none would compare to the night we lost our 6-year-old granddaughter in a car accident. There may not have been blood connecting her and I, but love did.

There I sat, on my knees in the flower garden, in the early morning a few days later. The dew was still on the roses, on her rose. I did not know where else to go. Her red rose planted for her namesake was blooming so much earlier than ever before. Before all of the pain and questions and what ifs. She was so thrilled to think a rose was named after her, Sierra Rose. In reality, it was named before her, but that didn't matter. Her grandpa planted a rose named after her. But now she was gone from the earth and her rose was blooming on.

Did you know dew is a symbol of resurrection (Isaiah 26:19)? "Just as the earth brings forth its dew, so also it shall bring forth the dead to new life." Dew is a symbol of the redeemed and resurrected people of God. Because Jesus lives, so does Sierra. So can I, and so can you.

There were these little heart moments where I realized He could handle my grief, my questions, and my pain. I did not have to pretend or hide them. But I also had to heal. Many don't want to heal. Maybe they are afraid it means they will forget. The hardest thing to do is keep living without part of you. But we must allow God to heal our hearts. He is willing, always. Even in the middle. Actually, more than ever in the middle of our disappointments and heartache, we can ask God to show us the joy and peace and promises all around us.

> *"Great faith is a product of great fights.*
> *Great testimonies are the outcome of great tests.*
> *Great triumphs can only come out of great trials."*
> Smith Wigglesworth

The bottom line- God can and will use every one of our losses, betrayals, times of persecution, and pain. He will use them to change us, to mold us, and not only us but people and places around us, too. He did not cause them, because He is not the author of destruction and death. But He can and will use it all.

I witnessed so many of those moments the day and months after, and still do 9 years later. Watching our family heal. What the devil meant for evil, God can and often will use for good (Genesis 50:20).

But what causes moments, seasons, and times like this? Free will. But also, we have a real enemy. Scripture says, "he roams around seeking whom he may devour." But many things are consequences of our actions, or lack of action, or are out of our control because of the actions of others around us. That's when we hear the word "unfair" come out. Life is not always "fair." Live long enough and you learn that. But what does fair mean anyway? I can tell you this it means something different to the world than it does God. Ultimately, justice is His. And in the end, it will be "fair." Earthly fair is formed by emotions. It's a feeling meant to keep us trapped.

Dew collects gradually. It's not a rushing rain that floods. It comes in the quiet, and almost invisibly. It is known to help keep things alive in harsh conditions.

Often in morning, just before sunrise, when it is the lowest air temperature of the day, is the time when the dew point temperature is most likely to be reached. The moisture evaporating into the air from the soil saturates the air around the grass. Many don't even notice. It's that gradual.

What am I saying?

Sometimes, we heal gradually, too. But God is always working, even when we can't see it. He doesn't neglect our broken hearts. His mercy is new every morning.

If the grief you're feeling has you feeling confused, then take a break and journal these things out. And remember, Heaven is real. It's glorious, and it's so much better than here. So, if we truly believe that, often our grief is from simply missing someone we love. And over missing our plans, and the way we thought our life would look. That's natural. It's ok. But don't let it hold you back. Because I know Sierra Rose is in heaven and she is cheering for her twin sister Meadow to live out her purpose. Cheering for her grandpa to plant more roses. Cheering for her momma and daddy and brother to live happy, abundant lives, and do what they are still here to do for God's glory.

Ask Holy Spirit to guide you:

1. Am I truly confused? (unable to think clearly; bewildered)
2. Write down how you really feel, raw and real. Next, remember this most important fact, God is not the author of confusion (1 Corinthians 14:33). Jesus is the Prince of Peace.
3. Next, remember, He will give peace even in the unknowing or waiting moments. He never withholds peace. We can step away from it, but He doesn't take it away.

Sierra Rose

Stop and smell the roses...

- Roses are one of the oldest flowers in existence, with fossils being found that date back 35 million years.

- Roses grow around the world, and there are said to be around 150 different species, and all are edible.

- Roses come in many colors and scents. Their lovely aroma is the most popular scent for perfume-making all around the world.

- Roses have sparked creative minds for centuries in poetry and art around the world.

- The rose is the national flower of the Unites States of America.

The rose is my favorite flower. We have grown many types from shrub, miniature, to my favorite hybrid tea. While I am no expert, here are some of my own rose gardening tips:

- Roses love sunshine. They need a spot that guarantees at least 6 hours of sun a day (early sun preferably).

- Roses need well-draining soil, and do best with 12 inches of mulch around the base.

- I water at the base of the plant heavily, twice a week, during the hot dry season. They like a good, deep watering more than sporadic sprinkles.

- I also use a rose fertilizer in the early spring and late fall.

- Disease and pests are a learning curve. You have to find what's right for you.

- Frequent pruning of smaller, weak limbs, and deadheading bloomed out flowers will help the plant grow stronger.

19

Live in the now

*"and to make it your ambition to lead a quiet life: You should
mind your own business and work with your hands, just as
we told you, so that your daily life may win the respect of
outsiders and so that you will not be dependent on anybody."*
1 Thessalonians 4:11-12

I used to say things like, "I was born in the wrong time
period," or, "I wish we could go back to simpler times."
I have always loved old things and living history. While
there is nothing wrong with learning from history, and
many things that have been dated are actually timeless
(like gardening, working with your hands, slowing down
and savoring a meal by candlelight, reading a real book
not on screens), the bottom line is: we are born and live in
this time and place for a Godgiven purpose. He has a plan.

One day, I was praying, and the Lord asked me to
stop saying those things. He asked me to embrace, live,
and trust Him with why I am here now. I had never
thought of it as dishonoring or creating a place in mind

for contempt. But in many ways, it does. If we long for things to look and be different than they are, we doubt God has a reason and plan for us where we are now. We are physically in places as well as part of places in time. What does that mean? Well, I am physically in my house, and I have lived in many physical homes in my life. But we are meant to fully live in each one. I am also physically in a town, state, and nation. Which may look different than other places both seasonally and demographically. But I am also part of a time period and culture. Which also looks different than other time periods and cultures. And no time period or culture is "simpler." It may look like it, but really, it's not. Why am I saying this?

Because God knew when and why I would be living, and you, too. He is not surprised by the technology or sin or disunity, or of the scary fact that bread can sit on a shelf for 2 weeks without molding. He knew everything we would be up against, and yet, here we are.

So, what should we do? Ask Him to show you why personally. But also spend some time in the Word. It's alive, and packed full of instruction. He is speaking. And believe me when I say, you were born for such a time as this (Esther 4:14)!

The truth is, some timeless things like working with our hands, minding our own business, and being a good example to those around us have not changed. Therefore, go into the whole world. Embrace your time with a happy heart. What an honor it is to co-labor with the Lord, and to be His hands and feet to a hurt, dying, scared world. Don't forget that.

You can learn a lot

of things from the flowers.

-Aluce in Wonderland

20

Arise, beloved

"Awake o sleeper and arise from the dead,
and Christ will shine on you."
Ephesians 5:14

There is a danger to spiritual sleep, like apathy (lack of enthusiasm, interest, or concern). But we can't allow ourselves to be swallowed up in that. We must allow the hope and faith we have in God to reveal and awaken His bride. We don't go to war for Him, we go with Him. And guess what? He already won. So that means we fight from victory not for victory! Realizing that is everything! He is asking for you to co-labor with Him!

"For we are God s coworkers; you are God s field,
you are God s building."
1 Corinthians 3:9

He isn't coming back for a bride that is hiding or hunkered down in a bunker, no. Or complaining about how evil and dark the world is (that should not shock you)! He is coming back for a warrior bride!

We are called to help find the lost sheep and bring them home. It's a rescue mission, not a self-preserving one.

"Radical Christianity" shouldn't even be a phrase that sets Christians apart. We are called to be set apart from the world, not each other. That's radical in itself.

One morning, I felt the Lord remind me of my great grandma (she was born in 1900). I was 11 when she died. I can still remember her playing her piano, worshiping the Lord in the middle of day when I would ride my bike to her house. She loved God, her family, and her community. But one phrase stuck with me the most. It took me years to realize why.

She said, "He isn't coming back until the whole world hears the good news. There is still work to be done." *(from Matt 24:13)*

This woman lived through the Great Depression, World Wars, and normal-life pain and loss. But she never stopped sharing the gospel with how she lived her life, which was a mostly quiet life spent working with her hands. She never stopped praying. She didn't give up because the world was dark and full of evil. She knew her God loved the whole world. So, even if the news made it all look like it was over, she knew the truth:

It's not over until He says it's over.

Why do I say all this? Because it's still true today. The harvest is great, but the workers are few! This world is dark, and that's not new. Not one bit new. But remember: the devil can't create a thing. So, he uses the same tactics over and over and over.

"So shall they fear The name of the Lord from the west,
And His glory from the rising of the sun;
When the enemy comes in, like a flood
The Spirit of the Lord will lift up a standard against him."
Isaiah 59:19

There is a stirring; do you feel it? It's taking place all around the earth; the bride of Christ is waking up. And she knows this battle is the Lord's, and He already won. She knows she has been given all authority! The warrior bride knows this battle is not against flesh and blood but Hell. She doesn't seek glory for her own name, but desires to honor and glorify the name of Jesus. She is spotless, without blemish or wrinkle, and she isn't cowering in a corner!

So now, more than ever, we need to arise with her, as one! Unity is key! And shine brighter than ever. How? Simple (notice I didn't say easy): do what Jesus says.

do not merely listen to the word, and deceive
yourselves… do what it says.
James 1:22-25

Jesus is the word made flesh
John 14

Back up to John 2:5. Mary, the mother of Jesus, tells them, "do whatever Jesus says to do." What does He say? Here is a short version:

"a new command I give you: love another. As I have loved you, you must love one another."
John 13:34

"Religion that is pure and undefiled before God, the Father, is this: to visit orphans and widows in their affliction, and to keep oneself unstained from the world."
James 1:27

"heal the sick, raise the dead, cleanse those with leprosy, drive out demons. Freely you have received, freely give."
Matthew 10:8

"all authority in heaven and on earth had been given to me. Therefore GO and make disciples of all nations, baptizing them in the name of the father, son and the Holy spirit, and teaching them to obey everything I have commanded you."
Matthew 28:16-20

Pray with me:

Lord, we come boldly to your throne of grace. We come with everything we have... our trauma, our hurts, disappointments, sin, failures. And also with our goals, our desires, and every single thing we did well, too.

We know that apart from Christ there is nothing good, anyway. We leave it at the foot of the cross, and we ask you to remind us if we try to pick it up again. We remove labels and name tags given to us by this world, and as we lay it all down, we arise warriors. We know the battle is Yours and You have already won! So, each day, we live with an understanding that we co-labor with You to share the good news of Jesus Christ all around this world! In Jesus' name we pray, amen.

Lastly, I asked the Lord once about why had that one phrase stuck with me more than anything else she had said. And He said, "Because of the call on your life to the nations." It was a seed. Planted in good soil, watered over time by many, and weeded later on in life, too. But ultimately, the Lord made it grow.

Her legacy, of love and faith and prayer, outweighs all the other stuff that tried to kill the seed. It outweighs the alcoholism, the religion, and the pain in my family. It outweighs my own big and small mistakes and failures and all the heartbreak.

Maybe you didn't have anyone like that. Maybe your whole life has been pain and trauma and defeat.

Well, guess what?

You have a new family now.
Welcome!
My legacy is yours, too.
We are adopted into a royal family, as our father is a King!
We get to start from clean, and go from glory to glory.
Believe that.

21

*"O Lord, all my longing is before you;
my sighing is not hidden from you."*
Psalm 38:9

Finding rest in the working and waiting is not what I'm good at. I can work and I can rest, and I can even wait. But one particularly hard day, I heard the Lord say, "I made you to do all three at once." I was like, "What? How? That's not possible!"

In this season of unlearning and relearning what rest means to God, just, wow… it's not the same as the world teaches, I can tell you that! It's not even the same as most Christians (not all) teach. Probably because we are on the same journey of unlearning and relearning, at some level.

BUT God. Right!? He is so good and so full of grace and mercy. And sometimes, rest actually looks (or feels) like work, moving forward, taking the one lighted step in front of you without knowing what's ahead (Psalm

119:10). The rest part comes in the knowing, in the believing God has already made the way. He is before you, and behind you (Psalm 139:5).

While watering my flower garden one morning in the late summer heat, I said, "Lord, this is work, not rest." Then I looked down and saw a bluebird feather and the peace that really does surpass all understanding washed over me. I felt rest in the reminder that He is always faithful and what He says will come to pass.

If you want the flowers (or fruit), you have to water the garden.

22

"If you want to know the secrets of a man, sit down and eat with him."

African proverb

There I stood, khaki grandma capri pants (I can say that, my grandma has a pair) and sandaled feet in the reddest dirt I had ever seen to date, staring at this beautiful, purple flowering tree. I was wondering when, and honestly how, I got here this fast. 41 years like blinking, all flashed before my eyes.

When my momma and I walked around Laura Ingall's Wilder house one summer vacation, I knew I would be a writer.

The first time I stood at the ocean's edge. The raw force of the waves and wind were only controlled by God Himself. Feeling so small, but also so alive.

My first day of high school I remember thinking this would be the longest 4 years of my life. It wasn't.

When I held my first baby, he was struggling to breathe, and I was praying to God to strengthen him and keep him alive. He did.

The day I said, "I will" to a life with the best man I've ever known.

The day my sister took her last breath, and the rainbows that popped up all over the sky were like a reminder that God's peace surpasses all understanding. It does.

All of it led and sculpted me into the woman standing in the red dirt of a foreign nation staring in wonder at the Jacaranda tree for the first time.

Jesus.

He is the only explanation. My only prayer, and make it yours today, too, is that they find me "exceeding their expectations." That they say of me, "she gave herself first to the Lord, and then, by the will of God, to us, also."

God is speaking. Will you listen?

Some ways God speaks:

- God speaks through scripture (2 Timothy 3:16-17). This is why reading the Word for yourself is so important. It really will change you. It is truth, and the only way truth can set you free is by using it to replace lies.
- God speaks through creation (Psalm 19:1-2).
- God speaks through the Holy Spirit (John 14:26).
- God speaks through dreams and visions (Joel 2:28).
- God speaks through His prophets and the gift of prophecy (you and me).
- God speaks through teachers (Romans 12:6-8).

It's important to remember, He can speak however He chooses, but He will not contradict His Word (Job 33:14). He doesn't confuse, steal, lie, or bring shame. Even in correction, He is love. Ask Him to speak to you. His Word says:

"Call to Me, and I will answer and show you great and hidden things that you have not known."
Jeremiah 33:3

23

"Delight yourself in the Lord and He will give you the desires of your heart."

Psalm 37:4

Okay, who here gets tired of the misuse of scripture or misunderstanding of scripture? I see those hands!

Well, in my mind I do! Ha! Mine is raised, too. This is one of those scriptures that used to bother me to see misused. Often, it is used to justify our "wants" and selfish indulgences and behaviors. Let's break it down, because God does care about what we desire when those desires are pure. When our desires are for our good and the good of others. When they align with His kingdom plans. Therein lies the key: purity of heart matters.

Our Father gives good gifts. But He is not a genie in a lamp. What does 'delight yourself in the Lord' even mean? It means you find pleasure and satisfaction in His presence, in His creation, in His word, and in sharing it with others. You find pleasure in healthy relationships (I truly believe God made us to need each other), enjoy all the blessing found in Him, and from that place, I truly believe anything is possible. Jesus says:

"Ask and it will be given to you; seek and you will find; knock and it will be opened to you. For everyone who asks receives, and the one who seeks finds and to the one who knocks it opened."
Matthew 7:7-8

"Whatever your ask in My name this I will do, that the Father may be glorified in the Son. You may ask me for anything in My name and I will do it! If you love Me obey My commandments."
John 14:13-15

Pray with me:

Lord, purify my heart and my desires. Align them with Your kingdom plan. Help me to delight in You, the way you delight in me. Thank You, Lord, for meeting our needs, even the ones we don't realize we have. In Jesus' name, amen.

Psalm 24

The earth is the LORD's and the fullness thereof,
The world and those who dwell therein,
For He has founded it upon the seas
And established it upon the rivers.

Who shall ascend the hill of the LORD?
And who shall stand in His holy place?
He who has clean hands and a pure heart,
Who does not lift up his soul to what is false and does
not swear deceitfully.
He will receive blessing from the LORD and
righteousness from the God of his salvation.
Such is the generation of those who seek Him, who seek
the face of the God of Jacob.

Selah

Lift up your heads, O gates! And be lifted up, O ancient
doors, that the King of glory may come in. Who is this
King of glory? The LORD, strong and mighty,
the LORD, mighty in battle!

Lift up your heads, O gates! And lift them up, O ancient
doors, that the King of glory may come in. Who is this
King of glory? The LORD of hosts, he is the King of glory!

Selah

24

Which path are you on?

"But I am afraid that your minds will be led astray from sincere and pure devotion in Christ."
2 Corinthians 11:3

Just like there is the ascending path that leads you higher and closer to the Lord, there is also a path that leads you away. It's not always overnight, but the wages of sin are always death. It's not always malicious rebellion or blatant sin. It can even look like something "good" at first, such as work, busyness, or even a hobby. Don't get me wrong, work and healthy hobbies aren't sinful. Where your priorities are is what matters to God. All throughout scripture we see the warnings, and the choice we have to make that will determine our eternal destiny. Even being lukewarm, neither hot nor cold, He says will get you spit out (Revelation 3).

In Psalms 1, we see one path leads to the righteous, and one leads to the wicked. Psalm 17 says there are two paths in front of the feet of men, one that leads to the Lord, and one leads to the destroyer. Jesus also tells us in Matthew 7 that there are two gates: the narrow gate which leads to life, and the wide gate with leads to destruction. He also tells us to build our life on the Rock, not the sand. And then in Matthew 13, He speaks about the wheat and the tares. Then, in Matthew 25, there are the sheep and goats.

Do you see the pattern?

You have a choice to make.

Will you take the invitation, and the ascending path that leads to life?

Jesus also warns that many will try and deceive you, and so make you think are on the right path (Matthew 7:15). That used to scare me. It used to make me feel hopeless, like no matter what I do I will miss it, or I will never be good enough. But that's a lie from Hell. Because Jesus also promises us that we will know His voice (John 19:27), and He sent us a helper named the Holy Spirit who indwells in those who believe (Romans 8:9).

The point is yes, we all have a choice to make. But if we posture our heart and follow Him, we won't miss it. Because He won't let you. How do we do that? Jesus calls it abiding in John 15.

Slow down, and spend some time with the Lord. Whatever that looks like for you. Read the Word.

Allow His Holy Spirit to fill you. Find a small group of likeminded healthy friends to do life with.

Scripture says that His Word is Spirit and truth and gives life, so just breathing it in will transform you. Remember, your salvation is a free gift, but intimacy with the Lord will cost you. The cost is worth it. It's all worth it. I promise.

My prayer for you:

That you will be so rooted in Christ. That you are like a tree firmly planted by streams of water, that yields fruit in all seasons, whose leaf does not wither, and whatever you do prospers (Psalm 1).

That you always choose the path to righteousness and run the race set before you with joy and peace.

That the only time you come back down the mountain, is to help rescue and equip others.

In Jesus' name, amen.

About the Illustrator

Artist Carmella Calhoun is a wife, mom, and nonna based just outside Nashville, TN. She works as a full-time artist in her "Creative Carmella" home studio specializing in jewelry design, painting, and illustration. From an early age, she has always been inspired by God's creation and uses this inspiration in her work daily. Flowers, birds, the light filtering through the trees... she has always been drawn to these things and can often be caught "painting pictures in her mind" of those very sights.

Her goal with her work has always been to add joy however and wherever she is able to.

You can follow along with her creative endeavors on Instagram at @creativecarmella or shop her website at www.creativecarmella.com

About the Author

Shannon R. Hess is a writer, homemaker, and missionary. But her favorite title is wife to Jim, and momma to three now grown children that live around the world. She lives in the Midwest, but spent most of her childhood moving around with her military family.

She loves flowers and words, especially the power the Word of God has to change and bring life. Shannon is also a writing coach and founder of House of Acts Press.

Other things written by Shannon include:

Dreaming With A Healthy Heart, a scripturally sound, in-depth book about how to dream with God. It has made it to over 7 nations and counting, and can be found on Amazon.

She also pens a monthly children's subscription letter called Grace Journeys.

You can also find her writings in The House of Acts Newsletter, and on her blog.

To find out more information about these things, and how to sign up, visit www.houseofactspress.com and www.shannonrhess.com

Shannon can also be found on Instagram and Facebook.

To my mother,

Thank you for always planting flowers no matter where
we lived and for planting hope in my heart.

www.ingramcontent.com/pod-product-compliance
Lightning Source LLC
Chambersburg PA
CBHW071719140626
46557CB00012B/971